Please, Wind?

Written by
Carol Greene

Illustrated by
Gene Sharp

Children's Press®
A Division of Scholastic Inc.
New York • Toronto • London • Auckland • Sydney
Mexico City • New Delhi • Hong Kong
Danbury, Connecticut

This book is for Emily.

Library of Congress Cataloging in Publication Data

Greene, Carol.
  Please, wind?

  (A Rookie reader)
  Summary: A child begs the wind to blow hard
enough to make a kite fly. Includes word list.
  [1. Winds—Fiction]   I. Sharp, Gene,
1923-   ill.   II. Title.   III. Series.
PZ7.G82845Pl   1982   [E]   82-4548
ISBN 0-516-02033-1   AACR2

It is still.

It is so still.

There is no wind.

Wind? Wind?

Blow!

Please, wind?

Listen.

It is a whisper.

A wind whisper.

Whisper, wind.

Whisper and grow.

Grow, grow…

and blow!

Oh!

Oh!

Blow butterfly and bird.

20

Blow cat and dog.

Blow...

hat!

And, wind?

Please blow kite.

Blow.

Blow!

Go.

Go!

There!

WORD LIST

		is	please
a	cat	it	so
and	dog	kite	still
bird	go	listen	there
blow	grow	no	whisper
butterfly	hat	oh	wind

About the Author

Carol Greene has written over 20 books for children, plus stories, poems, songs, and filmstrips. She has also worked as a children's editor and a teacher of writing for children. She received a B. A. in English Literature from Park College, Parkville, Missouri, and an M. A. in Musicology from Indiana University. Ms. Greene lives in St. Louis, Missouri. When she isn't writing, she likes to read, travel, sing, do volunteer work at her church—and write some more. Her *The Super Snoops and the Missing Sleepers* and *Sandra Day O'Connor, First Woman on the Supreme Court* have also been published by Childrens Press.

About the Artist

Gene Sharp has illustrated books, including school books, for a number of publishers. Among the books he has illustrated for Childrens Press are *The Super Snoops and the Missing Sleepers* and several in the "That's a Good Question" series.